Jealous
to
Death

Jealous to Death

JACQUELINE STEWART

authorHOUSE®

AuthorHouse™
1663 Liberty Drive
Bloomington, IN 47403
www.authorhouse.com
Phone: 1-800-839-8640

Published by AuthorHouse   08/22/2012

ISBN: 978-1-4772-3170-8 (sc)
ISBN: 978-1-4772-3169-2 (e)

Library of Congress Control Number: 2012911488

This book is dedicated to my mother, Deloris White and to my grandmother, Lillie Mae Frazier. You push me daily into the will of God for my Life. Thank you.

Acknowledgments

I would like to thank my parents for their constant prayers for my life. Your faith has helped me to get through trying times and seasons. To my loving husband and daughter Ahriel, I am forever appreciative of your love and support. I'm grateful to the Strength of my life, God my Father for giving me the ability to write. Without your Words, I am lost.

Table of Contents

Introduction xi

Chapter One: What is Disobedience? 1

Chapter Two: Rejected by the Spirit of the Lord 4

Chapter Three: Rejection Births Jealousy 7

Chapter Four: Rejection Births Anger 10

Chapter Five: Rejection Births Hate 14

Chapter Six: Rejection Births Manipulation 17

Chapter Seven: Rejection Births Lies and Deceit 20

Chapter Eight: Rejection Births Delusion 23

Chapter Nine: Rejection Births Denial 26

Chapter Ten: Rejection Births Death 30

Introduction

"And Samuel said, Hath the LORD as great delight in burnt offerings and sacrifices, as in obeying the voice of the LORD? Behold, to obey is better than sacrifice, and to hearken than the fat of rams. For rebellion is as the sin of witchcraft, and stubbornness is as iniquity and idolatry. Because thou hast rejected the word of the LORD, he hath also rejected thee from being king"—1 Samuel 15:22-23 (KJV).

Saul had been chosen by God to lead the people of Israel as king, but only two years into his reign he found himself being a hindrance to the kingdom of God. Saul many times disobeyed the instruction and Word of the Lord, which caused him to be rejected by the Spirit of the Lord. He continued to reign in his appointed position as king for thirty eight more years, but the Spirit of the Lord no longer resided with him. Basically he still had the job, but he no longer had the happiness and peace while doing it. God no longer had his back. Often times while reading the scriptures concerning Saul, I noticed that the Word of God still referred to Saul as being anointed throughout his reign. Matter of fact David twice had the chance to kill Saul (*1 Samuel 24 and 26*), but he didn't because even though Saul was rejected by the Spirit of the Lord, he was still anointed. I would ask God how could Saul still be anointed as king, yet was rejected by His Spirit? I realized that his anointing was on behalf of the people, meaning that he had been anointed to get the task done but he was no longer chosen. It is one thing when one has been hired just to get a job done, than when one has been hired because they have been chosen.

1 Samuel 16:14 says, "But the spirit of the LORD departed from Saul, and an evil spirit from the LORD troubled him" (KJV).

What is the Spirit of the Lord? It is the voice of God. Saul was rejected from hearing the voice of the Lord, and as we read through 1 Samuel, we see that the voice of God being void from his life took him to a place of consulting a witch (***read 1 Samuel 28:1-25***). Being without God, had gotten so bad for the king that he felt the need to consult the very abomination that he had once driven out from the presence of his people. Saul had become desperate. In this book I will discuss the meaning of disobedience, being rejected by the Spirit of the Lord because of disobedience and what being rejected by the Spirit of the Lord can cultivate in one's heart. Reading the story of Saul we see that he goes through several stages, and that several negative traits were birthed out of his heart. He went through the stages of jealousy, anger, hate, manipulation, lies and deceit, delusion and denial. All of which eventually brought him to his death. God doesn't want us to go through what Saul went through. All that He asks of His people is for obedience.

Chapter One

What is Disobedience?

Webster's dictionary defines disobedience as the refusal to comply or to disregard. Another word that Webster uses to define disobedience is the word transgress, which means to sin. Saul had a hard time following authority, boundaries, laws and commands and his attitude of defiance caused him to transgress against the Lord. Saul's first offense against the Lord was in *1 Samuel 13:1-14*, when he stepped in the role of priest to offer a burnt offering before the Lord. He knew that only priest were supposed to do this ritual, yet he chose to go against what had been set by God and felt compelled to do his own thing. Saul violates the decree of the Lord again in *1 Samuel 15:1-23* when he doesn't follow through by annihilating all that God had told him to kill concerning the Amalekites. Not only does he not follow through with the command of the Lord, but he lies about doing so. Have you ever heard the saying, "you dog me once shame on you, but if you dog me twice then shame on me?" God gave Saul another chance after his first mishap of disobedience, but after the second time it had gotten to a point of "not only is he disobeying me, but now he's lying along with the disobedience." He took God anointing and loving him for granted. He tried to take advantage of the situation. God knew that it was time to let Saul go. Listen to *1 Samuel 15:23*.

1 Samuel 15:23-"For rebellion is as the sin of witchcraft, and stubbornness is as iniquity and idolatry . . ." (KJV).

Saul had completely rebelled against the Word of the Lord, and the scripture above says that "rebellion is as the sin of witchcraft." That being said, Saul was acting like a witch. He wanted to manipulate the laws of God to fit his way of thinking and of doing things. How many of you know that God can't be manipulated, and that we can't change His Word? If we try to do so, then we're fighting a losing battle. The sentence of that verse goes on to say, "And stubbornness is as iniquity and idolatry." Saul had become stiff necked and stubborn, and as we see from this scripture, God first equates his stubbornness with iniquity. The word iniquity is defined as being a gross injustice to something or someone. Saul's disobedience was a gross injustice to the Lord.

Saint of God what a powerful term, and it shows us how violated God feels when we don't obey him. The Word of God also equates stubbornness with idolatry. What is idolatry? Idolatry is the worship of false gods. You may be thinking "what false gods was Saul worshiping?" Saul began to worship himself. He began to exalt his thoughts above God's. Every time he disobeyed the Lord, he was placing himself above God. Saul fiddled so much with the thought of being like God that he began to think he was God. He forgot the key word which is "like." Just because we are like God doesn't mean we are God. The same spirit the Devil had that decided to rise itself up against the sovereignty, power and intelligence of God was the same spirit that lied deep in the king's heart.

Sometimes we as God's people think of ourselves as being able to do a better job than someone else at our work place, church or where ever we are, but the truth is that it doesn't matter that you "think" you can do better because you haven't been given the authority to do whatever the task at hand is better. A lot of times we think that our way is better than God's so we try to push him out of the way, but we have to humble ourselves and remember that we will never be smarter than the Creator of the universe that has created all things, including us.

Isaiah 55:8-9 says, "For my thoughts are not your thoughts, neither are your ways my ways, saith the LORD. For as the heavens are higher than the earth, so are my ways higher than your ways, and my thoughts than your thoughts" (KJV).

God has been around since the beginning of time, and in fact He is the beginning of time, so it behooves us to know and understand that he has life all figured out. As we come back to the story of Saul, the Word shows us that he got so caught up in people praising him that he began to minimize the thoughts and the ways of Jehovah, the Lord his God. This brought him into a heart of disobedience, which brought about him being rejected by the Spirit of the Lord. Oh how I would hate to be rejected by the Lord's Spirit! Saul hated it too, and that's why when God's chosen David came on the scene Saul first loved him, then his love for David turned to hate. Continue to read, the Lord wants to either set you free and/or keep you free.

Chapter Two

Rejected by the Spirit of the Lord

"But the spirit of the Lord departed from Saul, and an evil spirit from the Lord troubled him"-1 Samuel 16:14 (KJV).

What does it mean to be rejected? The word reject is described as refusing to accept, consider or take for some purpose or use. It is also described as the refusal to hear or to receive. When the Spirit of the Lord departed from Saul, God had rejected to accept to use him for the purpose of being king over His people. He was no longer considered to be used for the purpose. The Lord no longer heard or received him or his prayers. Could you imagine no longer being accepted by God, refusing to be used for his purpose or him no longer hearing you; or even worse you no longer hearing him? What a horrible place to be in spiritually, so horrible that the prophet Samuel mourned for Saul. He mourned for his soul.

"And Samuel came no more to see Saul until the day of his death: nevertheless Samuel mourned for Saul: and the LORD repented that he had made Saul king over Israel"-1 Samuel 15:35 (KJV).

Not only did Samuel mourn for Saul, but the Word says that Lord repented of what He had made Saul, which was king over Israel. God had changed his mind towards Saul, and regretted that He had set him on high with such a position. Does God regret where he has placed you? I pray not. Have you forgotten that it is the Lord that has promoted you? Do you fully understand that in order for you to stay in the position that God has given you, you must obey? God loves us, but he won't tolerate sin. He won't tolerate our disobedience. The Word of the Lord goes on to tell us that even though Samuel continued to mourn for Saul, God was ready to move on to another vessel.

"And the LORD said unto Samuel, How long wilt thou mourn for Saul, seeing I have rejected him from reigning over Israel? Fill thine horn with oil, and go, I will send thee to Jesse the Bethlehemite: for I have provided me a king among the sons"-1 Samuel 16:1 (KJV).

God regretted His decision concerning Saul but He didn't sit around and mourn as did Samuel, the Lord was ready to move on to a king He had provided. Saints of God, our Creator understands timing, seasons and opportunities. He understands that there are things that have to get done. If you and I won't get them done how and when He we wants them to get done, then he will find someone that will. Some may think that God's attitude of "dropping" Saul and moving forward was harsh, but think about this . . . what employer wants to keep an employee that doesn't take heed and adhere to authority? If the employee won't get the job done and respect leadership, the employer will let the employee go and hire someone that will.

For some reason, we as people of God can act like God need us, but it's not that He needs you, He wants you. God delights in showing himself mighty through his creation. His glory shining up on us gives Him great joy, but it's up to us not to abuse that which God gives. If you have found yourself on the road of rejection by the Spirit of the Lord, repent and turn. God is waiting to be with you as you journey with Him down the avenue of obedience.

Chapter Three

Rejection Births Jealousy

Are you now jealous because God has rejected you from His presence and position, and now has chosen another? Saul definitely was jealous. Here it was a young, handsome and anointed man had come on the scene. He was only a sheep keeper, yet he had been chosen by God Almighty to do His work. He was David the Bethlehemite. He was skillful at playing the harp, so Saul hired him to be a part of his staff. Every time the son of Jesse would play the lyre, the evil spirit from the Lord that tormented Saul would depart from him. David went from keeping sheep to playing the harp for the king, from playing the harp for the king to killing a giant and from killing a giant to winning battles. God continuously promoted David, so the man that once loved him now became jealous of him.

"And the women answered one another as they played, and said, Saul hath slain his thousands, and David his ten thousands. And Saul was very wroth, and the saying displeased him; and said, They have ascribed unto David ten thousands, and to me they have ascribed but thousands: and what can he have more but the kingdom? And Saul eyed David from that day and forward"—1 Samuel 18:7-9 (KJV).

First Samuel uses the term "eyed." Saul jealously observed David within his heart. Even though David fought for him, stood by him and respected him, Saul's heart began to despise him. He wanted his name to be the only name to be made great. He didn't want to share the glory with any one, and when David was praised higher than Saul the Word says that Saul was displeased. Have you become displeased with another one's anointing? You could be sitting right next to them in church, working with them on a job or it could be a family member, and in your heart and mind you are displeased with them. You literally can't stand the favor of God that is on their life. You may be harboring jealous emotions but know that your jealousy isn't going to stop God from blessing someone else, and it's not going to manipulate Him into not withdrawing His hand from you.

The only thing that jealousy cultivates is bitterness, and if bitterness prolongs it will cultivate disease, and of course if disease stays long enough it will bring death. You may wonder what kind of death? You will find yourself mentally dead by not being able to see your future, spiritually dead by not being able to connect with God, emotionally dead by not being able to develop healthy and balanced relationships and physically dead by being plagued with cancers, high blood pressure, ulcers and a list of other deadly devices. Jealousy basically is only intimidating and killing you. Let's look at what the Word of God says about jealousy.

Proverbs 6:34 says, "For Jealousy is the rage of a man . . ." (KJV).

The deep emotion of rage has caused its carrier/s to either be killed or to kill. Have you ever seen those stories on television where someone killed another person because they wanted something that the other person had? They either wanted the person's spouse, job or social status. They were driven by jealousy. The consequence of being driven by this spirit only comes to disaster.

Song of Solomon 8:6 says, ". . . jealousy is cruel as the grave . . ."—(KJV).

Solomon parallels jealousy's cruelty with the grave. The grave is full of darkness and death, and so is the soul of this spirit. Pray and ask the Lord to remove Satan's grip from your life. He is trying to use jealousy as a tool to, as the old folk say, "kill two birds with one stone." The stone represents jealousy, and the birds represent you and the one you envy.

Chapter Four

Rejection Births Anger

"And it came to pass on the morrow, that the evil spirit from God came upon Saul, and he prophesied in the midst of the house: and David played with his hand, as at other times: and there was a javelin in Saul's hand. And Saul cast the Javelin; for he said, I will smite David even to the wall with it. And David avoided out of his presence twice"—1 Samuel 18:10-11 (KJV).

Here we see that Saul's attitude towards David went from jealousy to anger. He was angry about David's favor, so now he sought to greatly harm him. Saul used a javelin to try to smite David, but what are you trying to use to smite the one you're angered towards? His weapon was physical but yours maybe more on a spiritual, emotional or mental level. Are you trying to kill someone's soul? Maybe you're using the techniques of gossip, slander and lies or maybe you're using cruel forms of rejection in order to bring a person down to break their spirit. It doesn't matter what unseen weapon you're trying to use, all you know is that you're hoping to cause great harm, damage or even death.

I've learned that anger doesn't care of the destruction it causes, and if it's not happy then it doesn't want you to be happy. Saul's torment caused him to be unhappy with himself, with his position and with those around him, especially David. David's glow bothered him, and he was going to do all that he could in order to make the future king's light dim. I believe that Saul was really angry with himself more so than he was with David. "If I had only obeyed the voice of the Lord, then I wouldn't be in this condition" he thought. "If I had only not cared about the opinions of people more than the instruction of the Lord, then God would still be with me," said the king. Saul truly despised himself. Child of God if you're angry toward someone that hasn't done anything towards you, then there is something about yourself that you despise.

Psalm 37:8 says, "Cease from anger, and forsake wrath: fret not thyself in any wise to do evil."

The longer you stay in anger and wrath, the longer your mind will think on plans of evil. Saul's anger caused him to plot and scheme against David.

"And Michal Saul's daughter loved David: and they told Saul, and the thing pleased him. And Saul said, I will give him her, that she may be a snare to him, and that the hand of the Philistines may be against him. Wherefore Saul said to David, Thou shalt this day be my son in law in the one of the twain"—1 Samuel 18:20-21 (KJV).

The spirit of anger will use whatever and whomever it needs in order to get the job done. In this case, Saul's daughter was the bait. At this point, he cared about no one but himself. Anger will have your mind so clouded that you won't be able to see the pain that you're causing to those closest to you, and that actually love you.

Instead of stopping and thinking about his actions, Saul takes his scheme further.

"And Saul said, Thus shall ye say to David, The king desireth not any dowry, but an hundred foreskins of the Philistines, to be avenged of the king's enemies. But Saul thought to make David fall by the hand of the Philistines. And when his servants told David these words, it pleased David well to be the king's son in law"—1 Samuel 18:25-26 (KJV).

David couldn't believe that he was going to be the king of Israel's son in law. It was a great privilege to him, and he didn't want to take the opportunity lightly. Even though David's heart was pure towards him and Michal's soon to be marriage, his soon to be father in law's heart wasn't pure. Saul knew that David would do anything to have his daughter's hand in marriage, so he asked that David would bring him a hundred foreskins of the Philistines. Saul put David into harm's way hoping that the Philistines would kill him. Saul didn't have the "guts" to lay a hand on David; however he knew that the Philistine army would have the "guts." The great thing about the end of this story is that God didn't allow David to be defeated.

"Wherefore David arose and went, he and his men, and slew of the Philistines two hundred men; and David brought their foreskins, and they gave them in full tale to the king, that he might be the king's son in law. And Saul gave him Michal his daughter to wife"—1 Samuel 18:27 (KJV).

Angry man or woman of God, your anger doesn't have enough power to "take out" the anointing of God. Instead of being angry about what God has done or is doing in someone else's life, change the mind of your heart, change the way that you think and ask God to set you back on the path of righteousness.

Chapter Five

Rejection Births Hate

"And Saul was yet the more afraid of David; and Saul became David's enemy continually"—1 Samuel 18:29 (KJV).

The Word says that Saul became David's *enemy* continually. An enemy is someone that seeks to injure and overthrow. An enemy is someone that is an adversary. Saul without ceasing tried to injure and overthrow David. Nonstop he sought to contend with him. He continuously opposed David because he hated him. Why did Saul very much hate David? He hated him because he feared him. What was there to fear about David? The Word of the Lord says in *1 Samuel 18:14-15* that Saul feared David because he behaved himself wisely.

Are you mad because the one you hate won't come down to your level, and fight you back? You've used weapons of lies, gossip, slander or whatever weapon of your choice against them, and they refuse to come back at you in the same manner. Instead of repaying evil for evil, they choose to forgive, love and walk forward in the will of God. People could tell that David was different by how he treated those around him. Saul knew that David was special because of the way that he reacted to the way that Saul acted towards him. Like I said previously, David twice had the chance to take Saul's life but he chose not to. How many people do you know if had the

14

chance to kill their enemy wouldn't take that chance? There aren't many people that are that gracious in the world today. It takes the Love of God in order for us to behave in the way that David did towards Saul.

Going back to the verse above, it says that Saul *feared* David. What does the Word of God say about fear?

1 John 4:18 says, "There is no fear in love; perfect love casteth out fear: because fear hath torment. He that feareth is not made perfect in love" (KJV).

Saul didn't have true love for God, and that's why he wouldn't obey him (look at *John 14:15*). He didn't have respect (love) for David, and that is why he tried to kill him. Saul was void of love, and that is why he was tormented with fear. One could even say that the *evil spirit* that tormented Saul was a spirit of fear. This spirit came up on him because of his disobedience, and God was trying to teach Saul that He was God and that there was no other God above Him. God was trying to teach Saul to revere Him (honor and respect Him). If you're in hate (fear) towards God's anointed, God is trying to teach you to revere Himself as Lord. Grab on to spiritual insight, and take the time to be taught. The Holy Spirit wants to teach you.

Leviticus 19:17 commands us, "Thou shalt not hate thy brother in thine heart: thou shalt in any wise rebuke thy neighbor, and not suffer sin upon him (KJV).

God commands us to not to hate one another. He doesn't want us to be jealous of our brother or angry with our sister. He doesn't want us to be in competition for his attention or for a position and as a result we murder one another, but He wants us to prefer each other above ourselves (look at ***Romans 12:10***). Children of God if you walk in the obedience of God then you can walk in the peace, faith, confidence, assurance and the love of God. If you obey him, then there will be no doubt in your mind that He has your back. The Word says blessed are those that trust Him. How do we show the King of kings that we trust Him? We show our trust through our obedience.

Chapter Six

Rejection Births Manipulation

"And Saul spake to Jonathan his son, and to all his servants, that they should kill David"—1 Samuel 19:1 (KJV).

Saul became manipulative. He tried to manipulate others in to joining in on his plot to kill David. He even tried to use David's good friend, Jonathan to be a part of his scheme. Have you come to a place of trying to manipulate others, even the friend/friends of the anointed to do your dirty deeds? Here it is that you may have found yourself trying to do whatever you can, and use whomever you can to set up God's chosen. You're trying to control the situation by saying hateful things about the person in order to get others to hate them too. You figure if you're not alone in your ploy then maybe the job can get done, and you'll send them running. Servant of the Lord what you need to understand is that the righteous are never intimidated by your ugly looks, giant like body movements or any other gimmicks you may have. Though they look helpless, God has connected them with one that will not turn their back on them to sell them out.

"But Jonathan Saul's son delighted much in David: and Jonathan told David, saying, Saul my father seeketh to kill thee: now therefore, I pray thee, take heed to thyself until the morning, and abide in a secret place, and hide thyself: and I will go out

and stand beside my father in the field where thou art, and I will commune with my father of thee; and what I see, that I will tell thee"—1 Samuel 19:2-3 (KJV).

Jonathan was David's friend, but he was also Saul's son. I'm sure he was placed in a hard predicament, but Jonathan chose righteousness over relationship. Jonathan watched out for David, and he revealed to him time and time again Saul's plan/s to kill David so that David could run to safety. Jonathan possessed something that his father did not, and that was reverence for God, the people of God and the things of God.

"And Jonathan spake good of David unto Saul his father, and said unto him, Let not the king sin against his servant, against David; because he hath not sinned against thee, and because his works have been to thee-ward very good: for he did put his life in his hand, and slew the Philistine, and the LORD wrought a great salvation for all Israel: thou sawest it, and didst rejoice: wherefore then wilt thou sin against innocent blood, to slay David without a cause?"—1 Samuel 19:4-5 (KJV).

Jonathan spoke on behalf of David. He reminded his father of the good that David did for Israel. He had enough sense to know that Saul laying his hand on David to kill him would be a sin. He tried to get Saul to rationalize and see that it wasn't David in the wrong, but the king himself. He let Saul know that you're trying to kill my friend without a cause. I'm here to let you know that you're trying to kill the anointed without a cause. They haven't done a thing to you, yet you don't like them. They smile at you, speak to you and say hello, yet you can't stand them. I urge you to never lay your hand on someone without a cause.

Proverbs 26:2 says, "As the bird by wandering, as the swallow by flying, so the curse causeless shall not come" (KJV).

Saint of God though you speak your curse words on another, and try to rally up your troops just know that all that you're doing shall be of no effect because the Word of God says that an undeserved curse has no effect. You don't have to feel like you have to manipulate others in order to get what you want. Humble yourself and follow Jehovah Jireh, He is willing to give you the good of the land.

Chapter Seven

Rejection Births Lies and Deceit

Jonathan, Saul's son and David's friend pleaded with Saul on behalf of David. He reminded Saul of all the good that David had done for the kingdom. His words began to calm his father and Jonathan thought, "Finally Saul is thinking reasonably."

"And Saul hearkened unto the voice of Jonathan: and Saul sware, As the LORD liveth, he shall not be slain. And Jonathan called David, and Jonathan shewed him all those things. And Jonathan brought David to Saul, and he was in his presence, as in time past. And there was war again: and David went out, and fought with the Philistines, and slew them with a great slaughter; and they fled from him"—1 Samuel 19:6-7 (KJV).

Jonathan was sure that he had bridged the gap between his father and his best friend. Saul accepted David back into his presence without doing him any harm, and on top of that Saul had even made a vow unto the Lord that he wouldn't try to kill David. I'm sure Jonathan felt pleased. Here it is that once again David is back teamed up with Saul fighting wars, and killing the Philistine army in great multitudes. David felt relieved and happy to be back in the presence of the king . . . so he thought.

"And the evil spirit from the LORD was upon Saul, as he sat in his house with his javelin in his hand: and David played with his hand. And Saul sought to smite David even to the wall with the javelin; but he slipped away out of Saul's presence, and he smote the javelin into the wall: and David fled, and escaped that night"—1 Samuel 19:9-10 (KJV).

Saul lied to Jonathan and to the Lord. He made a vow to God that he wouldn't try to kill David, but he knew the entire time in his heart that receiving David back into his presence would give him another opportunity to take David's life. Saul was a liar and he was deceptive. He was slipping further and further away from the truth. Have you too like Saul have slipped further and further away from the truth? Have you now become a liar? Are you walking in the evil spirit of deception? You've accepted the one you hate only waiting to have the opportune time to kill them. You've pretended to be a friend. You've pretended to love them with your hugs and nice words. You may be fooling the one you oppose, but you're not fooling God.

Jeremiah 17:9 says, "The heart is deceitful above all things, and desperately wicked: who can know it? I the LORD search the heart, I try the reins, even to give every man according to his ways, and according to the fruit of his doings. As the partridge sitteth on eggs, and hatcheth them not; so he that getteth riches, and not by right, shall leave them in the midst of his days, and at his end shall be a fool" (KJV).

Saul thought that the lies of his heart would not be exposed, but eventually they were. Beloved of God, the Father of heaven and of earth discerns the intentions of our hearts. We are repaid according to the fruit of our hearts. If you gain that in which you want by lies and deception, sooner or later you will find yourself empty handed. Child of the Most High, you don't have to lie and deceive to get what you want. God loves you and wants to bless you. His Word says that He is no respecter of persons, and what He has done for another, He is also happy to do for you. Don't continue to let your heart go down an evil path. Obey Jehovah God; He is waiting to lavish you with the desires of your heart.

Chapter Eight

Rejection Births Delusion

"And Saul said unto him, Why have ye conspired against me, thou and the son of Jesse, in that thou hast given him bread, and a sword, and hast inquired of God for him, that he should rise against me, to lie in wait, as at this day"—1 Samuel 22:13 (KJV).

Saul's constant pursuit of David caused him to become delusional to the point that he thought that any one that helped David was against him, and was his enemy. In this instance, he felt as if though Ahimelech a priest of Nob had gotten with David and conspired against him because Ahimelech inquired of the Lord for David, and gave David provisions as well as the sword of Goliath the Philistine. Even though Ahimelech and the other priests were not conspiring against the king by helping David, in Saul's mind he thought that they were. He then made it be so that David's help was his enemies. Matter of fact, Saul wanted to make David's help his enemies. He hated them because they were in connection with the one he hated. Have you ever walked in that kind of attitude or are you walking in that kind of attitude? Where you don't like "James" just because he in some way has helped "Phil" the one you can't stand? Your dislike for James is without a cause just like your dislike for Phil is without one. James is only an innocent bystander to your anger towards Phil, and now you seek to annihilate James along with your seeking to annihilate Phil. Your mind has become crazy, filled with false perceptions and Delusions. Just like your current state of mind, Saul's mind was set on Devour mode.

"Then Ahimelech answered the king, and said, And who is so faithful among all thy servants as David, which is the king's son in law, and goeth at thy bidding, and is honourable in thine house? Did I then begin to inquire of God for him? Be it far from me: let not the king impute any thing unto his servant, nor to all the house of my father: for thy servant knew nothing of all this, less or more"—1 Samuel 22:14-15 (KJV).

Here it is that Ahimelech is afraid because he recognizes Saul's anger. He had no idea that Saul's heart had changed towards David, and that now the king was against David instead of being for him. Ahimelech was baffled! He tells Saul that the only reason why he helped David was because David was one of Saul's most faithful servants, as well as he was Saul's son in law. In Ahimelech's mind he thought who more to bless than David, he's been most faithful to the king of Israel. Ahimelech had no idea of what was going on. He didn't know that he was doing "wrong" by helping Israel's future king, David. Ahimelech's explanation didn't matter to Saul. He only saw the situation how he wanted to see it. He became as a "mad cow."

"And the king said, Thou shalt surely die, Ahimelech, thou, and all thy father's house. And the king said unto the footmen that stood about him, Turn, and slay the priests of the LORD; because their hand also is with David, and because they knew when he fled, and did not shew it to me"—1 Samuel 22:16-17 (KJV).

Saul was so out of his mind that he sinned against the Lord by slaying Ahimelech and eighty five other priests of Nob. If you read further (***verse 20***), you will see that Saul also slays the citizens of Nob. He slayed men, women, children and babies; he didn't even leave out the animals. His mind was unstable and out of control. Servant of the Lord disobedience unto God your father will cause you to become unstable and out of control. You're unstable because you can no longer hear from the Lord because He has removed His spirit from you. Obey him daughter, obey him son; we need the voice of the Lord to lead and guide us to places of peace, and from places of danger. Just like you're seeking to devour another, the enemy is seeking to devour you. Obedience is the key to ease your troubled mind.

Chapter Nine

Rejection Births Denial

Merriam Webster's dictionary tells us that denial is the refusal to admit the truth or reality. Saul had come to a place in life where he had a hard time seeing, and admitting truth and reality. He wouldn't admit to himself as well as to the ones that followed him that the Lord had departed from him. If you go back to *1 Samuel 15:30* you will see that even though the spirit of the Lord departed from Saul, and he knew it that he still wanted Samuel to honor him before the elders as if the Lord was still with him. He was in denial. I believe that Saul was surprised of the Lord's departure. After all, he was the king of Israel. I can hear Saul saying, "How dare He leaves me; all that I've done for His kingdom! This is the kind of thinking that says the Lord owed Saul something. The truth was that the Lord had blessed Saul with power, and he felt like he had the authority to abuse it. I can see Saul slaying those who wouldn't follow him, yet he himself wouldn't follow the Lord.

Are you feeling like you are above the Lord's instructions? When one disobeys sound instruction, they feel as if though they are above what has been instructed. They think that they know best. They don't want to follow, feel as if though they don't have to follow and are stubbornly not going to follow. Just like Saul, in the end you will find that not adhering to the instructions of God will cost you more than adhering to His instructions.

Going back to the story of Saul, we see that Saul wanted to hear the voice of The Lord. He was in Denial that the Lord was no longer speaking to him; therefore he cultivated his voice to sound like the voice of God.

"1 Samuel 23:7 says, "And it was told Saul that David was come to Keilah. And Saul said, God hath delivered him into mine hand; for he is shut in, by entering into a town that hath gates and bars. And Saul called all the people together to war, to go to Keilah, to besiege David and his men" (KJV).

If you go back and Read the beginning of this chapter, you will see that the Philistines had gone down to Keilah to fight againt the city. David heard of what the Philistines had done, and inquired of the Lord if he should go down to aid Keilah by fighting against the Philistines. The Lord told David and his men to go to Keilah for He would deliver the Philistines into their hands. David defeated the Philistines and saved Keilah. Saul heard of David being in Keilah, and he believed that God had given him the opportunity to kill David. Why would Saul think that God, who had clearly taken His voice from him had delivered his anointed servant David into his hands? Why would Saul think that God was willing to give him victory over His chosen king? Why would Saul even feel or think that he heard from the voice of the Lord that David was in a position and place to be defeated? Simply because Saul had fostered and trained his voice to sound like God's voice, but there was no truth, no power or no God in the voice he heard.

David found out that Saul was coming down to Keilah to kill him, and the Lord even told David that the very people that he just saved out of the hands of the Philistine's would deliver him up into the hands of Saul. The people of Keliah were going to hand David over to Saul, but the Lord delivered him. David escaped from the city, and from the wrath of Saul. Now, who do you think truly heard from the voice of the Lord? The god of Saul (Saul's mind) predicted David's defeat, but it didn't happen. The God of David helped him to once again defeat the Philistines, as well as helped him to flee from a deathly situation concerning Saul.

Saul continuously found himself in a mind of denial. He even continues to pursue David, and there was another group of people the Ziphites who were willing to hand David over to Saul. Saul once again thinks that the Lord is for him, because in his mind the Lord has put David in another position and place to be captured and killed.

"And Saul said, Blessed be ye of the LORD; for ye have compassion on me. Go, I pray you, prepare yet, and know and see his place where his haunt is, and who hath seen him there: for it is told me that he dealeth very subtilly"—1 Samuel 23:21-22 (KJV).

Saul calls the people blessed and of the Lord because they were willing to give him what he wanted, which was the life of David. He felt as if the Ziphites were an answered prayer from the Lord. How could they be an answered prayer from the Lord if the prayers of Saul were not even heard? Saint of God disobedience causes your prayers to go unheard. They're only hitting a glass ceiling, and never meeting the ears of God. How can you go to the alter of God to ask Him of anything, yet you won't obey what He's asking you to do? You quote the Word of God, but you won't obey it. God is looking for obedient servants. He wants to work miracles through the universe. If you have fostered your voice in to sounding like God's voice, I pray that you would quickly turn from your state of denial.

Chapter Ten

Rejection Births Death

"Then said Saul unto his armourbearer, Draw thy sword, and thrust me through therewith; lest these uncircumcised come and thrust me through, and abuse me. But his armourbearer would not; for he was sore afraid. Therefore Saul took a sword, and fell upon it"—1 Samuel 31:4 (KJV).

Saul had lived his last thirty eight years as the king of Israel in disobedience, rejection by the Lord's spirit, Jealousy, anger, hate, manipulation, lies and deceit, delusion, denial and they all brought him to his death. Saul was in the battle field void of the peace of God, and was very afraid. He knew that he was about to be defeated by the group of people that he had defeated so many times in times past. He knew that the Lord wouldn't hear his prayer and come to his aid because spiritually wise he was all alone. This battle wouldn't be his for the taking for his time was up. Fear closed in on him and he felt as if though he only had one option and that was to take his own life.

Child of God disobedience will only lead to spiritual death which will cause you to feel like you only have one option, which is physical death. Disobedience will turn your soul into a wicked dark person filled with jealousy, anger, hate, manipulation, lies and deceit, delusion and denial. You will find yourself acting in ways that you never thought you could or would act, and in the end you will be in a place of misery.

Saul could've easily turned from walking away from the Lord, but he chose not to. Time and time again he sinned, lied and wouldn't repent. I beseech you child of God don't be like Saul. Go back, and find that place where you got off track, where you disobeyed and stopped heeding to the Father's voice. Go back to the time where you realized that you no longer heard him, but the voice of your own mind instead. If you go back, realize and repent He will forgive you.

1 John 1:9 says, "If we confess our sins, he is faithful and just to forgive us our sins, and to cleanse us from all unrighteousness" (KJV).

He wants to forgive us of our sins, and cleanse us from all unrighteousness. He is a God of love, and he wants you to be blessed and not cursed. He wants you to be above and not beneath. He's for your success but you have to obey His voice, His Word and His commands. *Leviticus 26:3-13, Deuteronomy 7:12-24 and Deuteronomy28:1-14* tells us of our rewards for obedience. The enemy wants to deceive you into believing that God just wants to tell you what to do while He's hanging out on the throne, but that's a lie. Pride, rebellion and disobedience is why Satan was cast down from heaven and from the presence of the Lord. Misery loves company. Let the enemy know that you will no longer walk in darkness, but in God's everlasting light.

Let's pray:

Lord, I thank you that you are faithful and just to forgive me, and to cleanse me from all of my unrighteousness. I confess my sins, and admit that I have been walking down a disobedient path. Lord I turn back to you because I know that there is no other way, but through obedience of your will and your way. I love you Father for delivering me from the hands of wickedness. In Jesus' name I pray. Amen.

Contact Information:

Phone: (318)-581-2997

Email: jacquelinestewart1447@yahoo.com

Printed in the United States
By Bookmasters